HOW TO PROVOKE YOUR TESTIMONIES

"….for the testimony of Jesus is the spirit of prophecy."

Rev19:10

By
Franklin N. Abazie

How to Provoke your Testimonies

COPYRIGHT 2018 BY Franklin N Abazie
ISBN: 978:1-945-133-74-9
All right reserved. This book or any portion thereof may not be reproduced or used in any manner whatsoever without the express written permission of the publisher, except for the use of brief quotations in a book review. All Bible quotes are from King James Version and others as noted.

Published by: F N ABAZIE PUBLISHING HOUSE---
a.k.a,
Empowerment Bookstore:

That I may publish with the voice of thanksgiving and tell of all thy wondrous works. **Psalms26:7**

To order additional copies, wholesales or booking: Call the Church office (973-372-7518)
or Empowerment Bookstore Hotline 973-393-8518
Worship address:
343 Sanford Avenue Newark New Jersey 07106
Administrative Head Office address:
33 Schley Street Newark New Jersey 07112
Email:pastorfranknto@yahoo.com
Website www.fnabaziehealingministries.org
Publishing House: www.fnabaziepublishinghouse.org

This book is a production of F N Abazie Publishing House.

A publication Arms of Miracle of God Ministries 2018
First Edition

CONTENTS

THE MANDATE OF THE COMMISSION...........iv

ARMS OF THE COMMISSION............................v

INTRODUCTION...viii

CHAPTER 1

1. What are testimonies? 19

CHAPTER 2

2. The Joy of testimonies..26

CHAPTER 3

3. Prayer of Salvation...49

CHAPTER 4

4. About the Author..59

THE MANDATE OF THE COMMISSION

"THE MOMENT IS DUE TO IMPACT YOUR WORLD THROUGH THE REVIVAL OF THE HEALING & MIRACLE MINISTRY OF JESUS CHRIST OF NAZARETH.

I AM SENDING YOU TO RESTORE HEALTH UNTO THEE AND I WILL HEAL THEE OF THY WOUNDS, SAID THE LORD OF HOST."

ARMS OF THE COMMISSION

1) F N Abazie Ministries-Miracle of God Ministries (Miracle Chapel Intl)

2) F N Abazie TV Ministries: Global Television Ministry Outreach.

3) F N Abazie Radio Ministries: Radio Broadcasting Outreach.

4) F N Abazie Publishing House: Book Publication.

5) F N Abazie Bible School: also called Word of Healing Bible School (W.O.H.B.S)

6) F N Abazie Evangelistic Ass: Miracle of God Ministries: Global Crusade

7) Empowerment Bookstore: Book distribution.

8) F N Abazie Helping Hands: Meeting the help of the needy world wide

9) F N Abazie Disaster Recovery Mission: Global Disaster Recovery.

10) F N Abazie Prison Ministry: Prison Ministry for all convicts "Second chance"

Some of our ministry arms are waiting the appointed time to commence

FAVOR CONFESSION

Father thank you for making me righteous and accepted through the blood of Jesus Christ. Because of that, I am blessed and highly favored by God. I am the subject of your affection. Your favor surrounds me as a shield, and the first thing that people see around me is your favored shield.

Thank you that I have favor with you and man today. All day long people go out of their way to bless me and help me. I have favor with everyone that I deal with today. Doors that were once closed are now opened for me. I receive preferential treatment, and I have special privileges, I am Gods favored child.

No good thing will he withhold from me. Because of Gods favor my enemies cannot triumph over my life. I have supernatural increase and promotion. I declare restoration to everything that the devil has stolen from my life. I have honor in the midst of my adversaries and an increase in assets, especially in real estate and expansion of

Because I am highly favored by God, I experience great victories, supernatural turnarounds, and miraculous breakthrough in the midst of great impossibilities. I receive recognition, prominence, and honor. Petitions are granted to me even by ungodly authorities. Policies, rules, regulations, and laws are changed and reverse on my behalf.

I win battles that I don't even have to fight, because God fights them for me. This is the day, the set time and the designated moment for me to experience the free favor of God, that profusely and lavishly abound on my behalf in Jesus name. Amen.

INTRODUCTION

"I will speak of thy testimonies also before kings, and will not be ashamed." **Psalms119:46**

It is important that we all testify of the goodness of God. God is committed to add yet another testimony in our life, as long as we are willing to talk about it in the public.

"Whosoever therefore shall be ashamed of me and of my words in this adulterous and sinful generation; of him also shall the Son of man be ashamed, when he cometh in the glory of his Father with the holy angels." **Mark8:38**

This small book is a book of testimonies. It is written *"Bind up the testimony, seal the law among my disciples."* **Isaiah8:16.**

It is our core responsibility as Christians to share and keep sharing our testimonies with everyone as long as we live. Nobody knows you until someone introduces you to another person.

This entire book is all about the testimonies of Jesus Christ. As believers, we must key into the testimonies of others, if we desire God to give us our own testimonies in life.

The psalmist said *"Incline my heart unto thy testimonies, and not to covetousness."* **Psalm119:31.**

It is my prayer for you to key into the testimonies you will read in this book. The truth is, that is the only secret to get your own testimony.

David said *"I have stuck unto thy testimonies: O Lord, put me not to shame."* Every believer must know how to key into testimonies in life. Unless you talk about it will not be permanent for you.

"Jesus saith unto him, Thomas, because thou hast seen me, thou hast believed: blessed are they that have not seen, and yet have believed."

"For whosoever shall be ashamed of me and of my words, of him shall the Son of man be ashamed, when he shall come in his own glory, and in his Father's, and of the holy angels." **Luke9:26**

HIS DESTINY WAS THE CROSS....

HIS PURPOSE WAS LOVE.....

HIS REASON WAS YOU....

"Whosoever therefore shall be ashamed of me and of my words in this adulterous and sinful generation; of him also shall the Son of man be ashamed, when he cometh in the glory of his Father with the holy angels."

Mark8:38

"For whosoever shall be ashamed of me and of my words, of him shall the Son of man be ashamed, when he shall come in his own glory, and in his Father's, and of the holy angels."

Luke9:26

Encounter Prayer Points

"If ye shall ask any thing in my name, I will do it.." **John14:14**

Holy Spirit of God frustrate and disappoint, every one that is against my life and family, in the name of Jesus.

Father Lord destroy every demonic networks and traps against my progress in life in the name of Jesus.

Fire of God, destroy every demonic projection and curses against my life and destiny in the name of Jesus.

Every spell and curses pronounced against my destiny, break, in the name of Jesus.

Hand of God cage every power militating against my rising in life, in the name of Jesus.

Power of God silent every voice raising a counter motion against my elevation,

Blood of Jesus neutralize every spirit of Balaam hired to hinder my life, ministry, and career, the name of Jesus.

Fire of God destroy every curse that I have brought into my life through ignorance and disobedience, break by fire, in the name of Jesus.

Ancient of day destroy every power harassing my ministry in the name of Jesus.

Father God deliver me from invincible forces militating against my life and destiny.

Power of God frustrate every coven and demonic network, designed to frustrate and hinder my success in life, in the name of Jesus.

I dismantle every strong hold designed to imprison my talent in the mighty name of Jesus.

I reject every cycle of frustration, in the name of Jesus.

Power of God paralyze every agent assigned to frustrate my life in the name of Jesus.

Finger of God, grant me supernatural speed against all my contenders in the name of Jesus.

By the blood of Jesus, I destroy every familiar spirit caging my life and career.

Fire of God arrest every demonic agents, assigned to police my destiny and marriage.

By the blood of Jesus, I proclaim no weapon fashioned against me shall ever prosper.

Holy Spirit of God break me through and forward in life in the mighty name of Jesus.

God, smash me and renew my strength, in the name of Jesus.

Holy Spirit, open my eyes to see beyond the visible to the invisible, in the name of Jesus.

Father Lord grant me strength and power in the name of Jesus

O Lord, liberate my spirit to follow the leading of the Holy Spirit.

Holy Spirit, teach me to pray through problems instead of praying about, it in the name of Jesus.

Father Lord, deliver me from the false accusation in life, in the name of Jesus

By the blood of Jesus, every evil spiritual padlock and evil chain hindering my success, be roasted, in the name of Jesus.

By the blood of Jesus I rebuke every spirit of spiritual deafness and blindness in my life, in the name of Jesus.

Father Lord, empower me to dominate the enemy of my destiny in the name of Jesus.

Jesus Christ of Nazareth, heal my infirmities in the name of Jesus

Lord, anoint my eyes and my ears that they may see and hear wondrous things from heaven.

Father Lord, anoint me with power and authority to dominate all my enemies in the name of Jesus.

Fire of God roast every giant rising up against my life and career.

Holy Spirit of God destroy all my oppressors in the name of Jesus.

Angels of good new, bring my good news to me in the mighty name of Jesus.

Every strong man holding me down, lose your hold now in the name of Jesus.

I nullify every demonic prediction over my life in the name of Jesus.

By the blood of Jesus, I flush out every polluted deposit of the enemy in my life.

By the blood of Jesus, I paralyze every enemy of my promotion in the name of Jesus.

Father Lord, destroy any power tormenting my life that is not from you.

Holy Ghost fire, ignite the fire of revival in my life.

By the blood of Jesus, I declare victory over every conflicting trial

By the Blood of Jesus, I command the arrest of every demonic spirit, militating against my life

By the blood of Jesus, I proclaimed the blood of Jesus, over every device of the enemy.

By the blood of Jesus, I revoke stagnation and hardship over my life in the name of Jesus.

Holy Ghost fire, destroy every satanic arrangement in my life, in the name of Jesus.

CHAPTER 1
What are Testimonies?

"Whosoever therefore shall be ashamed of me and of my words in this adulterous and sinful generation; of him also shall the Son of man be ashamed, when he cometh in the glory of his Father with the holy angels." **Mark8:38**

Testimonies are the acts of God. It is the hand of God upon any prevailing challenge, or circumstance upon the life of man.

It is written, *"Because they regard not the works of the Lord, nor the operation of his hands, he shall destroy them, and not build them up."* **Psalms28:5.**

Every time you give a testimony of what God has done in your life, you set yourself up for the next testimony. The Lord said *"I did them suddenly, and they came to pass."*

In the business world, most small businesses use the word of the mouth to advertise a particular product or about a unique restaurant. In the kingdom of God, it is called testimony. Every time you talk about what God have done, it converts unbelievers.

Every time you share what God is doing in your life, it gives the unbeliever, yet, another opportunity to accept Jesus Christ as their personal Lord and savior. I like to say that, testimonies are the breathing ground for healings, and miracles.

As long as you share your testimony, God is pleased to do more miracles for you. Every time Jesus heals. The healing belongs to us, but the testimony belongs to Jesus. Every time you share your testimony, you give God the glory.

One woman in John chapter four, drew over five thousand men to the kingdom of God.

Chapter 1 - What are Testimonies?

"I have rejoiced in the way of thy testimonies, as much as in all riches." **Psalm 119:14**

"Thy testimonies also are my delight and my counselors." **Psalm 119:24**

"I have stuck unto thy testimonies: O Lord, put me not to shame. "I will speak of thy testimonies also before kings, and will not be ashamed." **Psalm 119:46**

Your testimony is not mere self-gratification, but it must come out of a pure heart, with the right intention. Often some folks try to steal the testimony of Jesus Christ. The truth is testimonies does not belong to the church or to the pastor, it belongs to God.

Often some of us want to share how well, and strong we can accomplish things in life.

It is written *"But by the grace of God I am what I am: and his grace which was bestowed upon me was not in vain; but I laboured more abundantly than they all: yet not I, but the grace of God which was with me."* **1cor15:10**

How do I build a life full of testimonies?

We must fill our spiritual life with prayer.

A life of prayer is a life of victory. Every time we pray we must believe that it is done. Spending time in His presence gives us all the courage, and boldness required to stand out and testify in the public. We must constantly search the scriptures. Unless you search the Holy Scripture, you will be missing out. There are things written in the bible concerning us, we must discover it. You cannot talk much about anyone who you do not know. If you must talk about Jesus, then you must know more about him through the Holy Bible

Chapter 1 - What are Testimonies?

We must constantly search the scriptures.

Unless you search the Holy Scripture, you will be missing out. There things written in the bible concerning us, we must encounter it. You cannot talk about anyone who you do not know. If you must talk about Jesus, then you must know more about him through the Holy bible.

We must be humbled enough to serve and help others.

It is written *"Jesus said unto him, Thou shalt love the Lord thy God with all thy heart, and with all thy soul, and with all thy mind. This is the first and great commandment. And the second is like unto it, Thou shalt love thy neighbour as thyself."* **Mathew22:37-39**

You must become a soul winner.

It is written *"The fruit of the righteous is a tree of life; and he that winneth souls is wise."* **Proverb11:30.**

Like as above, *"he that winneth souls is wise."* For the effectiveness of our testimony, we must become a soul winner for the kingdom of God. We must testify to others about our experience with the Lord Jesus.

It is one thing to talk about what God has done in our life. But it is another thing to talk about how good the Lord has been to us.

We must encourage other to repent and confess their sin. It is written *"Go ye therefore, and teach all nations, baptizing them in the name of the Father, and of the Son, and of the Holy Ghost."* **Matthew28:19**

"Jesus saith unto him, I am the way, the truth, and the life: no man cometh unto the Father, but by me." **John14:6**

Are you saved?

It is my prayer that you will make Jesus Christ the Lord of your life. Over the years, you have allowed so many people to have dominion and ruler ship over your life. It is time to turn over your entire life into the hand of God.

Chapter 2 - The Joy of Testimonies

Now repeat this Prayer after me

Say Lord Jesus, I accept you today, as my Lord and my savior, forgive me of my sins wash me with your blood. Right now, I believe, I am sanctified, I am save, I am free, I am free from the Power of sin to serve the Lord Jesus. Thank you Lord for saving me. Amen.

CHAPTER 2
The Joy of Testimonies

"He answered and said, Whether he be a sinner or no, I know not: one thing I know, that, whereas I was blind, now I see." **John 9:25**

If I may ask you, how do you feel whenever you win or succeed in what you have been striving to do? It is always a good feeling every time, we can testify of what God has done upon our life. O give thanks unto the Lord, for he is good: for his mercy endureth for ever.

In the opening scripture above, this blind man was super excited that all he wanted to say was that once he was blind now he can see. One of the reason favor and breakthrough stop flowing in our life is because we are not joyful.

Every time you lack the excitement to share your testimonies, it hinders the blessing of God from flowing into our lives.

Chapter 2 - The Joy of Testimonies

When Philip preached in Samaria, the bible recorded that there was joy in the city.

We must always embrace joy. Without the joy of testimony, we will lose touch with what God is doing, and wants to do in our lives. It is written *"Therefore with joy shall ye draw water out of the wells of salvation."* **Isaiah 12:3.**

We must always remain excited in life. Life is a special gift from God. God will not change because of our prevailing circumstances. Neither will God cease to be God because we fail to praise or thank Him.

"Because they regard not the works of the Lord, nor the operation of his hands, he shall destroy them, and not build them up." **Psalms 28:5.**

We must be excited and thank God for our life. Helen Keller said and I quote *"I cried because I had no shoes until I met a man who had no feet."* I encourage you to be excited for life is a gift.

Have you ever encouraged anyone to buy a product or eat in an outstanding restaurant that you recommended so strongly? Well, we must do the same thing in this kingdom. You must come into contact with powerful prayer ministries like **Miracle of God Ministries** for your total restoration and miracle in life. The great commission gives us the authority to tell everyone about the Lord Jesus Christ.

Share your conversion experience with everyone.

We must share how we became a born again Christian. Every time we share our testimony, we attract others to join the faith.

It is written, *"Go ye therefore, and teach all nations, baptizing them in the name of the Father, and of the Son, and of the Holy Ghost: Teaching them to observe all things whatsoever I have commanded you: and, lo, I am with you always, even unto the end of the world. Amen."* **Mathew28:19-20**

Chapter 2 - The Joy of Testimonies

It is written, *"Behold, the Lord's hand is not shortened, that it cannot save; neither his ear heavy, that it cannot hear: But your iniquities have separated between you and your God, and your sins have hid his face from you, that he will not hear."* **Isaiah59:1-2**

We must acknowledge that we are all sinner separated from God. Our *carnal nature* rebelled against the will and commandment of God. But it takes determination and dedication to live for Christ Jesus. Jesus Christ died and his blood was paid as a ransomed for the punishment for our sins.

We must have an active relationship with the Father

Do you pray? Do you love others?

After sharing our conversion experience, we must share our experience with the power of the gospel. I may sound blunt, but you must let others know the Lord. You must tell others of Jesus. We must constantly encourage people to come to the church with us, we must show them love and care.

"Thy testimonies have I taken as an heritage forever: for they are the rejoicing of my heart." **Psalms 119:111**

It is the joy of testimony to look around your friends and tell them of your encounter with the Lord Jesus. Although it is easier said than done.

Here is how you share your testimony.

1. Tell what your life was like before you met Jesus Christ.

Simply this should be a straight out story of how you encountered the Lord Jesus, and what He is doing in your life.

2. Share how Christ saved you.

Encourage someone with your born again experience. This is your story but it is for Gods glory to talk about it. Tell others of your life before and now, and glorify God for His goodness upon your life.

Chapter 2 - The Joy of Testimonies

3. Always confess your sins and proclaim Jesus Christ as the Lord over your life.

"For with the heart man believeth unto righteousness; and with the mouth confession is made unto salvation." **Romans10:10.**

God will never take the second place in your life. Unless you put him first, your testimony is incomplete. God must be first in all your story.

"Give glory to the Lord your God, before he cause darkness, and before your feet stumble upon the dark mountains, and, while ye look for light, he turn it into the shadow of death, and make it gross darkness." **Jer13:16.**

It is established *"I am the Lord: that is my name: and my glory will I not give to another, neither my praise to graven images."* **Isaiah42:8.**

4. Your relationship with God has been restored.

Embrace the life style of faith and live in the supernatural. It is written *"For God so loved the world that he gave his only begotten Son, that whosoever believeth in him should not perish, but have everlasting life."* **John3:16.**

God have restored your life, therefore always give him the praise and then glory. Otherwise you will incur a curse.

It is written *"And even as they did not like to retain God in their knowledge, God gave them over to a reprobate mind, to do those things which are not convenient;"* **Romans1:28.**

5. Tell everyone how the power of the gospel have changed your life.

For unless you share it they will not know of the power of the gospel. It is written *"For I am not ashamed of the gospel of Christ: for it is the power of God unto salvation to everyone that believeth; to the Jew first, and also to the Greek."* **Romans1:16.**

Chapter 2 - The Joy of Testimonies

Encourage everyone to seek first the kingdom of God and His righteousness, so that they will attract the addition that comes as a bonus.

"But seek ye first the kingdom of God, and his righteousness; and all these things shall be added unto you." **Mathew6:33.**

"While the earth remaineth, seedtime and harvest, and cold and heat, and summer and winter, and day and night shall not cease." **Genesuis8:22.**

"Cast thy bread upon the waters: for thou shalt find it after many days." **Eccl11:1.**

"Give a portion to seven, and also to eight; for thou knowest not what evil shall be upon the earth." **Eccl11:2.**

"If the clouds be full of rain, they empty themselves upon the earth: and if the tree fall toward the south, or toward the north, in the place where the tree falleth, there it shall be." **Eccl 11:3.**

"He that observeth the wind shall not sow; and he that regardeth the clouds shall not reap." **Eccl 11:4.**

I encourage you, to Share your testimony and watch my God decorate your life in Jesus Mighty Name.

Chapter 2 - The Joy of Testimonies

CONCLUSION

"....for the testimony of Jesus is the spirit of prophecy." **Rev19:10**

Every time you tell others about what God is doing in your life, God tell more people to come into favor and love with you. As long as your mouth is open God's hand is wide enough to fill it.

It is written, *"I am the Lord thy God, which brought thee out of the land of Egypt: open thy mouth wide, and I will fill it."* **Psalms81:10**

If you do not open your mouth to share your testimony the devil will. It is written *"And it shall turn to you for a testimony. Settle it therefore in your hearts, not to meditate before what ye shall answer: For I will give you a mouth and wisdom, which all your adversaries shall not be able to gainsay nor resist."* **Luke21:13-15.**

Any testimony belongs to Jesus Christ. No medical doctor, or lawyer should encourage you to tell others that he healed or helped you win that case. You must know the source of your victory. But truly no man can talk about him without being part of him

"Therefore if any man be in Christ, he is a new creature: old things are passed away; behold, all things are become new." **2cor5:17**

Now repeat this prayer after me;

Say Lord Jesus, I accept you today, as my Lord and my savior, forgive me of my sins wash me with your blood. Right now, I believe, I am sanctified, I am save, I am free, I am free from the Power of sin to serve the Lord Jesus. Thank you Lord for saving me. Amen.

Congratulations: YOU ARE NOW A BORN AGAIN CHRISTIAN

Chapter 2 - The Joy of Testimonies

What must I do to determine my divine visitation?

To determine divine visitation you must be born again. The word says as many as received him, to them gave He power to become the sons of God. Even to them that believe on his name.

To qualify for divine visitation do the following sincerely,

1) Acknowledge that you are a sinner and that He died for you. **Rom3:23**.

2) Repent of your sins. **Acts 3:19, Luke13:5, 2Peter3:9**

3) Believe in your heart that Jesus died for your sin. **Romans10:10**

4) Confess Jesus as the Lord over your life. **Romans10:10, Acts2:21**

Now repeat this Prayer after me

Say Lord Jesus, I accept you today, as my Lord and my savior, forgive me of my sins wash me with your blood. Right now, I believe, I am sanctified, I am save, I am free, I am free from the Power of sin to serve the Lord Jesus. Thank you Lord for saving me. Amen. Congratulations: YOU ARE NOW A BORN AGAIN CHRISTAIN

I adjure you to watch the Spirit of God bear witness with your Spirit confirming His word with signs following.

The word says The Spirit itself beareth witness with our spirit, that we are the children of God. Join a bible believing church or join us on our weekly and Sunday worship services at 343 Sanford Avenue Newark New Jersey 07106.

Chapter 2 - The Joy of Testimonies

WISDOM KEYS

Every Productive Society is a society heading to the top

Millions of Nigerians run away from Nigeria, very few Nigerians stay in Nigeria.

My decision to return Nigeria is the will of God for my life

My short coming in America after 18 years, trained me to be wise, to think, reflect and reason appropriately.

If you train your mind to reason it will train your hands to earn money.

It is absurd to use the money of the heathen to build the kingdom of the living God.

Every Ministry reveals its agenda and goal either at the beginning or at the end. Be careful of your life it is your first Ministry.

The average American mind is conditioned for a continual quest to get new things and (discard the former) and throw away old things.

When I considered well, my BMW jeep became my initial deposit for the work of the ministry in Nigeria

Everyone is waiting for you to change your mind until you change your thinking nothing changes around you.

Multiple academic degrees in other discipline gave me the chance to think, reflect and reason

What so everyone are thinking and reflecting at the moment reveals you to the time and the now factor

All events and intents are the product of precise thought processes, accurate reason every event is designed for a designated timeline

Wisdom is your ability to think, to create and invent. If you can think wise enough you will come out of penury

The distance between you and success is your creative ability to think reason and reflect accurate.

Chapter 2 - The Joy of Testimonies

Success is the result of hard work, commitment resolve and determination learning from past mistakes and failing.

If you organize your mind you have organized your life and destiny.

There is a thin line between success and failure. If you look above and beyond you are on your way to success.

Wealth is your ability to think, power is your ability to reason and success is your ability to be informed.

If you can make use of your mind by thinking and reasoning God will make use of your life and destiny.

Think and Be Great

Reflect, Reason, think and be great

Famous people are born of woman

That you will make it is your intention; that you will survive is your resolve, that you will succeed with changes is your determination, personal efforts and hard work.

No man was born a failure. Lack of vision is the end product of failure.

Working with mental patients encourages and aspire me to be a productive observant and dedicated to my assignment.

Successful people are not magicians, it is the will power combined with hard work, and determination and a resolve to succeed that make them succeed.

In the unequivocal state of the mind, intention is not a location or a position it is the state of the mind.

So many people think that they think. The mind is used to think reflect and reason. You will remain blind with your eye open until you can see with your mind by thinking.

There is no favoritism in accurate and precise calculation

Chapter 2 - The Joy of Testimonies

Although knowledge is power, information is the key and gateway to a great future.

It will take the hand of God to move the hand of man.

With the backing of the great wise God, nothing will disconnect you from your inheritance.

As long as you have wisdom and understanding of God, Satan and evil cannot manipulate your life and destiny.

You have come this far by yourself judgment and decision you have made in the past, now lean and listen to God for another dimension of greatness.

Great people are common people it is extra ordinary effort and the price of sacrifice that produces greatness.

As a mental direct care worker I saw a great pastor and a motivational speaker within myself.

Menial job does not reduce your self-worth, until you resolve to achieve greatness see greatness in all you do; you will never count in your community

The principle of Jesus will solve your gambling and addiction problems

The man of Jesus will lead you into heaven,

Everyone have their self-appraisal and what they think about you. Until you discover yourself other opinion about you will alter the real you.

Supervisors and directors are just a position in the chain of command in a work place. Never allow your supervisor hierarchy to alter your opinion about yourself.

Everyone can come out of debt if they make up their mind.

That I am not a decision maker at work does not diminish my contribution to my world.

Although it appears like it was a poor decision to accept a direct care employment at a psychiatric hospital as I reflect of my nine years of experience, it became apparent that I have learnt and experienced enough for my next assignment.

Self-encouragement and determination is a resolve of the heart.

Chapter 2 - The Joy of Testimonies

If you are determined to make a difference, and do the things that make a difference you will eventually make a difference.

Good things do not come easy

Short cuts will cut your life short.

Those who look ahead move ahead.

Life is all about making an impact. In your life time strive to make an impact in your community.

Make friends and connect with people who are moving ahead of you in life.

If you can look around well you have come a long way in your life, made a lot of difference and realized a lot of success in life.

If you are my old friend, hurry up to reach out to me before I become a stranger to you.

Everything I am blessed with inspirations from God, that change my definition and interpretation of the world around me.

I thought I was stagnant and lonely until I looked around and noticed my children running around and my wife cooking.

At 40 I resigned my Job to seek the Lord forever.

My ministry took a drastic rise to the top when the wisdom of God visited me with knowledge and understanding.

You will be a better person if you understand the characteristics of your personality – your mood swings attitudes and habits.

It is the seed of love you sow into the heart of a child and a woman that you reap in due time.

Love is not selfish, love share everything including the concealed secrets of the mind.

As long as you have a prayer life and a bible; you will never feel lonely, rejected and idle in the race of life.

When good friends disconnect from you, let them go, they might have seen something new in a different direction.

Confidence in yourself and in God is the only way to bring you out of captivity

Never train a child to waste his/her time.

The mind is the greatest assets of a great future.

Chapter 2 - The Joy of Testimonies

You walk by common sense run by principles and fly by instruction.

Those who fly in flight of life fly alone.

Up in the air you are alone. No one can toll you accept the compass of knowledge and information

I have seen a tolling vehicle I have seen a tolling ship I have never seen a tolling airplane.

I exercise my judgment and make a decision every minute of the day.

Decisions are crucial, critical and vital with reference to your future.

So many people wish for a great future. You can only work towards a great future.

Your celebrity status began when you discovered your talent. What are you good at? Work at it with all commitment.

Prayers will sustain you but the wisdom of God will prosper you.

When I met Oyedepo, his teachings changed my perspective, but when I met Ibiyeomie; His teaching changed my perception.

I will be successful in ministry if only I concentrate and focus my energy in the work of the ministry.

It took the late Dr. Vincent Pearle Norman's book to open my mind towards kingdom success.

CHAPTER 3
PRAYER OF SALVATION

"Neither is there salvation in any other: for there is none other name under heaven given among men, whereby we must be saved." **Acts4:12.**

Salvation means deliverance from sin and the destruction of the forces of the devil. Are you saved?

What must I do to determine my salvation?

To be saved we must be born again! The word says as many as received him, to them gave He power to become the sons of God. Even to them that believe on his name.

To qualify for divine visitation do the following sincerely,

1) Acknowledge that you are a sinner and that He died for you. **Rom3:23.**

2) Repent of your sins. **Acts 3:19, Luke13:5, 2Peter3:9**

3) Believe in your heart that Jesus died for your sin. **Romans10:10**

4) Confess Jesus as the Lord over your life. **Romans10:10, Acts2:21**

Now repeat this Prayer after me

Say Lord Jesus, I accept you today, as my Lord and my savior, forgive me of my sins wash me with your blood. Right now, I believe, I am sanctified, I am save, I am free, I am free from the Power of sin to serve the Lord Jesus. Thank you Lord for saving me. Amen.

Congratulations:

YOU ARE NOW A BORN AGAIN CHRISTAIN

Chapter 3 - Prayer of Salvation

The word says The Spirit itself beareth witness with our spirit, that we are the children of God.

MIRACLE CARE OUTREACH

"...But that the members should have the same care one for another" **1cor12:25**

We are all members of the body of Christ. Jesus commanded us to love our neighbor as ourselves. This includes caring for one another as a member of one body. True love is expressed in caring and giving. The word says for God so Love He gave….

Reach out to someone in need of Jesus, help someone in crisis find Christ. Look out and prove your love to Jesus by caring and inviting your friends and associates to find Jesus the Healer.

Invite your friends to our Home Care Cell Fellowship (Miracle chapel Intl Satellite fellowship) In the USA at 33 Schley Street Newark New Jersey 07112.

If you are in Nigeria—**MIRACLE OF GOD MINISTRIES**

**A.K.A "MIRACLE CHAPEL INTL"
Mpama –Egbu-Owerri Imo state Nigeria.**

(Home Care Cell fellowship Group). We meet every Tuesday at 6:00pm-7:00pm.

LIFE IS NOT ALL ABOUT DURATION BUT ITS ALL ABOUT DONATION

What does the above statement mean?....

"Life consists not in accumulation of material wealth.." **Luke12:15.**

"But it's all about liberality....meaning- what you can give and share with others." **Proverb11:25.**

When you live for others--You live forever- because you out live your generation by the legacy you live behind after you depart into glory to be with the Lord.

Chapter 3 - Prayer of Salvation

But when you live to yourself - you are reduced to self—you are easily forgotten when you die and depart in glory.

Permit me to admonish you today to live your life to be a blessing to a soul connected to you today. I want you to know that so many souls are connected and looking up to you, and through you so many souls will be saved and rescued from destruction. Will you disciple someone today to find Jesus Christ?

"As a genuine Christian; it is your duty to evangelize Jesus Christ to all you meet on your way. Jesus is still in the healing business-Jesus is still doing miracles from time of old to now.

Therefore tell someone about Jesus Christ today, disciple and bring them to Church." **John 1:45 Philip findeth Nathanael....**

Please to prove the sincerity of your love for God today; please become a soul winner. The dignity of your Christianity is hidden in your boldness to proclaim and evangelize Jesus Christ to all you meet on your way.

There is a question mark on the integrity of your Christianity until you become a life soul winner. Invite someone to join us worship the Lord Jesus this coming Sunday.

Amen

Chapter 3 - Prayer of Salvation

MIRACLE OF GOD MINISTRIES

PILLARS OF THE COMMISSION

We Believe Preach and Practice the following,

1) We believe and preach Salvation to every living human being

2) We believe and preach Repentance and forgiveness of sins

3) We believe and preach the baptism of the Holy Spirit and Spiritual gifts

4) We believe and teach the Prosperity

5) We believe and preach Divine Healing and Miracles (Signs &Wonder)

6) We believe and preach Faith

7) We believe and Proclaim the Power of God (Supernatural)

8) We believe and Proclaim Praise& Worship to God

9) We believe and preach Wisdom

10) We believe and preach Holiness (Consecration)

11) We believe and preach Vision

12) We believe and teach the Word of God

13) We believe and teach Success

14) We believe and practice Prayer

15) We believe and teach Deliverance

This 15 stones form the Pillars of Our Commission.

Become part of this church family and follow this great move of God.

MY HEART FELT PRAYER FOR YOU

It is my prayer that you testify today about the goodness of the Lord. I desire for you to have an encounter with our Lord Jesus Christ.

Chapter 3 - Prayer of Salvation

Now let me Pray for you:

Heavenly father give us a fresh testimony today. Lord do that which no man can do for us. And take all the glory. In Jesus mighty Name. Amen

Encounter with God

Unless you are left alone you are not ready to encounter God. Jacob was left alone and he encountered God. I strongly urge you to create a quiet time with your God. A time of meditation and reflection. God is still omnipotent and all powerful. But you have to discover this by prayer and meditation in the word of God.

Jacob encountered God

"And Jacob was left alone; and there wrestled a man with him until the breaking of the day. And when he saw that he prevailed not against him, he touched the hollow of his thigh; and the hollow of Jacob's thigh was out of joint, as he wrestled with him. And he said, Let me go, for the day breaketh.

And he said, I will not let thee go, except thou bless me. And he said unto him, What is thy name? And he said, Jacob. And he said, Thy name shall be called no more Jacob, but Israel: for as a prince hast thou power with God and with men, and hast prevailed." **Genesis32:24-28.**

Apostle Paul encountered God

"And as he journeyed, he came near Damascus: and suddenly there shined round about him a light from heaven:And he fell to the earth, and heard a voice saying unto him, Saul, Saul, why persecutest thou me?And he said, Who art thou, Lord? And the Lord said, I am Jesus whom thou persecutest: it is hard for thee to kick against the pricks." **Acts9:3-5**

CHAPTER 4
ABOUT THE AUTHOR

Rev Franklin N Abazie is the founding and Presiding Pastor of Miracle of God Ministries with headquarters in Newark, New Jersey USA and a branch church in Owerri- Imo State Nigeria. He is following the footsteps of one of his mentors, Oral Roberts (Healing Evangelist) of the blessed memory.

The Lord passed Oral Roberts healing mantle two days before he went to be with the Lord at age 91 into the hand of healing evangelist-Rev Franklin N Abazie in a vision.

In all his services the Power and Presence of God is present to heal all in his audience. He is an ordained man of God with a Healing Ministry reviving the healing and miracle ministry of Jesus Christ of Nazareth.

Pastor Franklin N Abazie, is called by God with a unique mandate:

"THE MOMENT IS DUE TO IMPACT YOUR WORLD THROUGH THE REVIVAL OF THE HEALING & MIRACLE MINISTRY OF JESUS CHRIST OF NAZARETH.

I AM SENDING YOU TO RESTORE HEALTH UNTO THEE AND I WILL HEAL THEE OF THY WOUNDS. SAID THE LORD OF HOST"

He is a gifted ardent Teacher of the word of God who operates also in the office of a Prophet, generating and attracting undeniable signs & wonders, special miracles and healings, with apostolic fireworks of the Holy Ghost.

He is the founding and presiding senior Pastor of this fast growing Healing ministry.

He has written over 86 inspirational, healing and transforming books covering almost all aspect of divine healing and life. He is happily married and blessed with children.

BOOKS BY REV FRANKLIN N ABAZIE

1) Commanding Abundance
2) The outcome of faith
3) Understanding the secret of prevailing prayers
4) Understanding the secret of the man God uses
5) Activating my due Season
6) Overcoming Divine Verdicts
7) The Outcome of Divine Wisdom
8) Understanding God's Restoration Mandate
9) Walking in the Victory and Authority of the truth
10) Gods Covenant Exemption
11) Destiny Restoration Pillars
12) Provoking Acceptable Praise
13) Understanding Divine Judgment
14) Activating Angelic Re-enforcement
15) Provoking Un-Merited Favor
16) The Benefits of the Speaking faith
17) Understanding Divine Arrangement

18) Understanding Divine Healing
19) The Mystery of Endurance
20) Obeying Divine Instructions
21) Understanding the Voice of God
22) Never give up on Hope
23) The prevailing Power of faith
24) Understanding Divine Prosperity
25) The Reward of Prayer
26) Covenant Keys to Answered Prayers
27) Activating the Forces of Vengeance
28) Put your faith to work
29) Where is your trust?
30) The Audacity of the Blood of Jesus
31) Redeeming Your Days
32) The force of Vision
33) Breaking the shackles of Family Curses
34) Wisdom for Marriage Stability
35) The winners Faith
36) The Prayer solution
37) The power of Prayer
38) Prayer strategy
39) The prayer that works
40) Walking in Forgiveness
41) The power of the grace of God

42) The power of Persistence
43) Overcoming Divine verdicts
44) The audacity of the blood of Jesus.
45) The prevailing power of the blood of Jesus
46) The benefit of the speaking faith.
47) Fearless faith
48) Redeeming Your Days.
49) The Supernatural Power of Prophecy
50) The companionship of the Holy Spirit
51) Understanding Divine Judgement
52) Understanding Divine Prosperity
53) Dominating Controlling Forces
54) The winners Faith
55) Destiny Restoration Pillars
56) Developing Spiritual Muscles
57) Inexplicable faith
58) The lifestyle of Prayer
59) Developing a positive attitude in life.
60) The mystery of Divine supply
61) Encounter with God's Power
62) Walking in love
63) Praying in the Spirit
64) How to provoke your testimony

65) Walking in the reality of the Anointing
66) The reality of new birth
67) The price of freedom
68) The Supernatural power of faith
69) The Power of Persistence
70) The intellectual components of Redemption
71) Overcoming Fear
72) The Force of Vision
73) Overcoming Prevailing Challenges
74) The Power of the Grace of God
75) My life & Ministry
76) The Mystery of Praise

MIRACLE OF GOD MINISTRIES

NIGERIA CRUSADE 2012

MIRACLE OF GOD MINISTRIES
NIGERIA CRUSADE 2012

MIRACLE OF GOD MINISTRIES

NIGERIA CRUSADE

2012

MIRACLE OF GOD MINISTRIES

NIGERIA CRUSADE

2012

www.ingramcontent.com/pod-product-compliance
Lightning Source LLC
Chambersburg PA
CBHW021451080526
44588CB00009B/790